LOS ANGELES CHARGERS

BRENDAN FLYNN

WWW.APEXEDITIONS.COM

Copyright © 2025 by Apex Editions, Mendota Heights, MN 55120. All rights reserved. No part of this book may be reproduced or utilized in any form or by any means without written permission from the publisher.

Apex is distributed by North Star Editions:
sales@northstareditions.com | 888-417-0195

Produced for Apex by Red Line Editorial.

Photographs ©: Aaron M. Sprecher/AP Images, cover, 1; Marcio Jose Sanchez/AP Images, 4–5, 58–59; Jeff Lewis/AP Images, 6–7; Shutterstock Images, 8–9, 40–41, 48–49, 54–55; Charles Aqua Viva/Getty Images Sport/Getty Images, 10–11; Michael Zagaris/Getty Images Sport/Getty Images, 12–13; Gene Puskar/AP Images, 14–15; Steve Grayson/Getty Images Sport/Getty Images, 16–17; Focus on Sport/Getty Images Sport/Getty Images, 19, 22–23; James Flores/Getty Images Sport/Getty Images, 20–21;Keith Srakocic/AP Images, 24–25; Stephen Dunn/Allsport/Getty Images Sport/Getty Images, 26–27; Rob Tringali/Sportschrome/Getty Images Sport/Getty Images, 28–29; Margaret Bowles/AP Images, 30–31; Jayne Kamin-Oncea/Getty Images Sport/Getty Images, 32–33, 38–39; Kevin Sabitus/Getty Images Sport/Getty Images, 34–35; Tom DiPace/AP Images, 37, 57; Patrick McDermott/Getty Images Sport/Getty Images, 42–43; Ryan Kang/Getty Images Sport/Getty Images, 44–45, 47; Jeff Gross/Getty Images Sport/Getty Images, 50–51; Doug Pensinger/Getty Images Sport/Getty Images, 52–53

Library of Congress Control Number: 2023922837

ISBN
979-8-89250-153-8 (hardcover)
979-8-89250-170-5 (paperback)
979-8-89250-294-8 (ebook pdf)
979-8-89250-187-3 (hosted ebook)

Printed in the United States of America
Mankato, MN
012025

NOTE TO PARENTS AND EDUCATORS

Apex books are designed to build literacy skills in striving readers. Exciting, high-interest content attracts and holds readers' attention. The text is carefully leveled to allow students to achieve success quickly.

TABLE OF CONTENTS

CHAPTER 1
BOLT UP! 4

CHAPTER 2
EARLY HISTORY 8

PLAYER SPOTLIGHT
DAN FOUTS 18

CHAPTER 3
LEGENDS 20

CHAPTER 4
RECENT HISTORY 28

PLAYER SPOTLIGHT
LADAINIAN TOMLINSON 36

CHAPTER 5
MODERN STARS 38

PLAYER SPOTLIGHT
JUSTIN HERBERT 46

CHAPTER 6
TEAM TRIVIA 48

TEAM RECORDS • 56
TIMELINE • 58
COMPREHENSION QUESTIONS • 60
GLOSSARY • 62
TO LEARN MORE • 63
ABOUT THE AUTHOR • 63
INDEX • 64

CHAPTER 1
BOLT UP!

The crowd is a sea of blue and gold. The fans rise to their feet. Music pumps through the stadium. Then, the Los Angeles Chargers run onto the field. It's time for football!

Chargers fans go wild as the players take the field.

Justin Herbert ran for 11 touchdowns in his first four NFL seasons.

The Chargers drive down the field. Quarterback Justin Herbert takes the snap. He doesn't see an open receiver. So, he starts running. He sprints into the end zone. It's a touchdown! Herbert is just getting started. He scores another touchdown later in the game. The star quarterback leads Los Angeles to a big win.

WHY THE BOLTS?

The Chargers have lightning bolts on the sides of their helmets. So, fans often use a nickname for the team. The Chargers have become known as the Bolts.

CHAPTER 2

EARLY HISTORY

The Los Angeles Chargers began playing in 1960. The team was an original member of the AFL. This league was separate from the NFL. The Chargers had a great first season. They won their division.

In their first season, the Chargers played at the Los Angeles Memorial Coliseum.

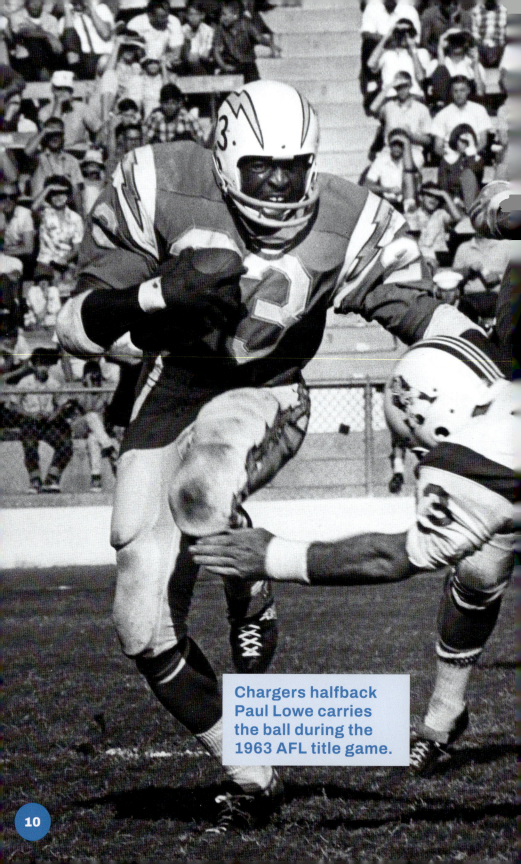

Chargers halfback Paul Lowe carries the ball during the 1963 AFL title game.

The Chargers didn't have many fans at first. Most people in the city cheered for the Los Angeles Rams. So, in 1961, the Chargers moved to San Diego. The team was a hit in its new city. The Chargers won four more division titles in the next five years. And in 1963, they won the AFL title. They crushed the Boston Patriots 51–10.

FIRST COACH

Sid Gillman was the Chargers' first head coach. He became known for his team's great offenses. Gillman often called passing plays. That made him a good fit for the AFL's wide-open style of play.

The AFL and NFL joined together in 1970. The Chargers became part of the AFC West division. The team's early NFL years didn't go well. But in 1978, Don Coryell took over as head coach. He led the team to three straight division titles. The Chargers also reached the conference title game two years in a row.

AIR CORYELL

Before Don Coryell arrived, most NFL teams relied on running. But Coryell changed that. His teams relied on passing. His style of play became known as Air Coryell. In his first six seasons, the Chargers led the NFL in passing yards.

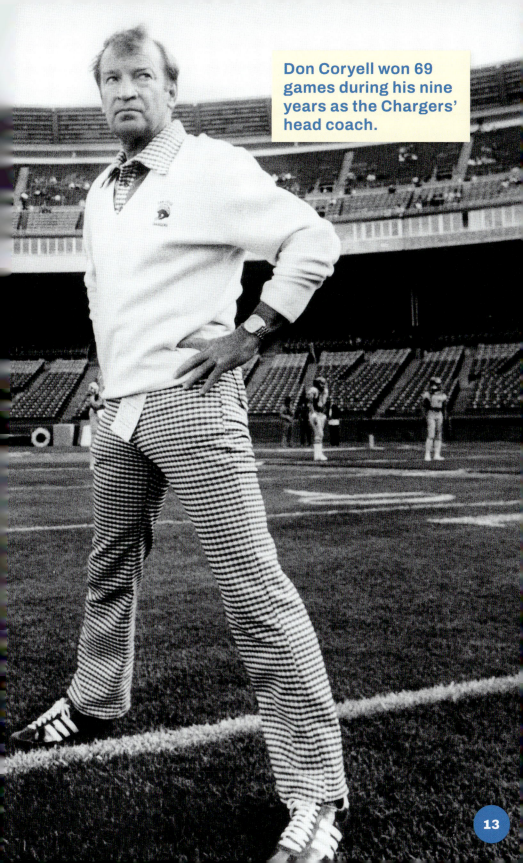

Don Coryell won 69 games during his nine years as the Chargers' head coach.

Stan Humphries attempts a pass in the conference title game against the Pittsburgh Steelers.

The Chargers hit another dry spell in the 1980s. Head coach Bobby Ross took over in 1992. In his first season, Ross led San Diego to a division title. The team went a step further in 1994. The Chargers reached their first Super Bowl. However, they lost to the San Francisco 49ers.

STAN THE MAN

In the 1994 season, the Chargers faced the Pittsburgh Steelers in the conference title game. San Diego trailed by 10 points in the third quarter. But Chargers quarterback Stan Humphries led a big rally. He threw two long touchdown passes. San Diego won 17–13.

San Diego went through another rough patch in the late 1990s. But fans had reason to be hopeful. In the 2001 draft, the Chargers picked two exciting players. One was running back LaDainian Tomlinson. The other was quarterback Drew Brees. In 2004, they led San Diego to its first division title in 10 years.

Drew Brees looks for an open receiver during a playoff game in the 2004 season.

PLAYER SPOTLIGHT

DAN FOUTS

A passing team needs a great quarterback to be successful. The Chargers selected Dan Fouts in the 1973 draft. Fouts was known for his powerful arm. He also had a quick release.

Fouts spent his entire 15-year career with the Chargers. He led the NFL in passing yards four years in a row. He was also the first player to top 4,000 passing yards three years in a row. Fouts ended up in the Pro Football Hall of Fame.

FOUTS THREW 254 TOUCHDOWN PASSES DURING HIS CAREER.

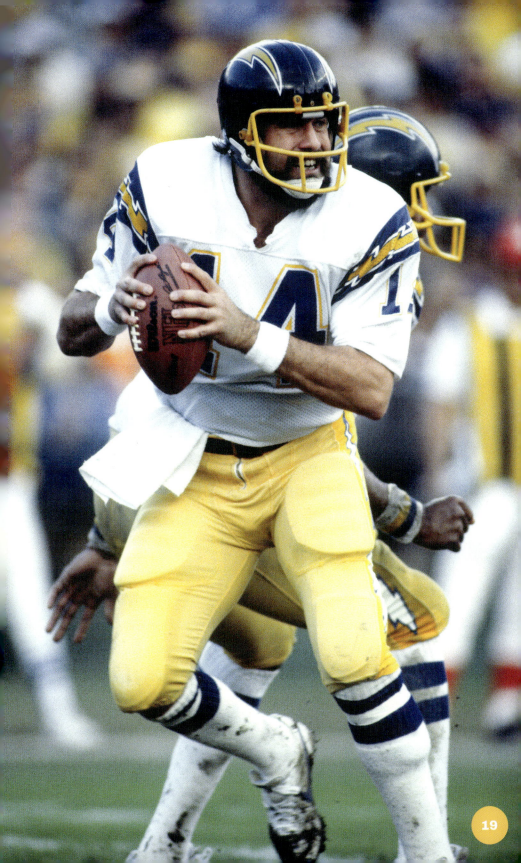

CHAPTER 3

LEGENDS

Quarterback John Hadl led San Diego's passing attack in the team's early years. Hadl spent 11 seasons with the Chargers. He led the AFL in passing yards twice in the 1960s. And he led the NFL in 1971. The Chargers traded Hadl away in 1973. That's when Dan Fouts arrived in San Diego.

John Hadl threw for 26,938 yards during his time with the Chargers.

The Chargers' quarterbacks have had many great targets over the years. Lance Alworth led the AFL in catches, yards, and touchdown catches three times. Charlie Joiner was known for his blazing speed and great moves. Tight end Kellen Winslow led the NFL in catches twice.

FAST START

In 1978, rookie John Jefferson led the NFL with 13 touchdown catches. He did it again two years later. The flashy receiver began his NFL career with three straight 1,000-yard seasons.

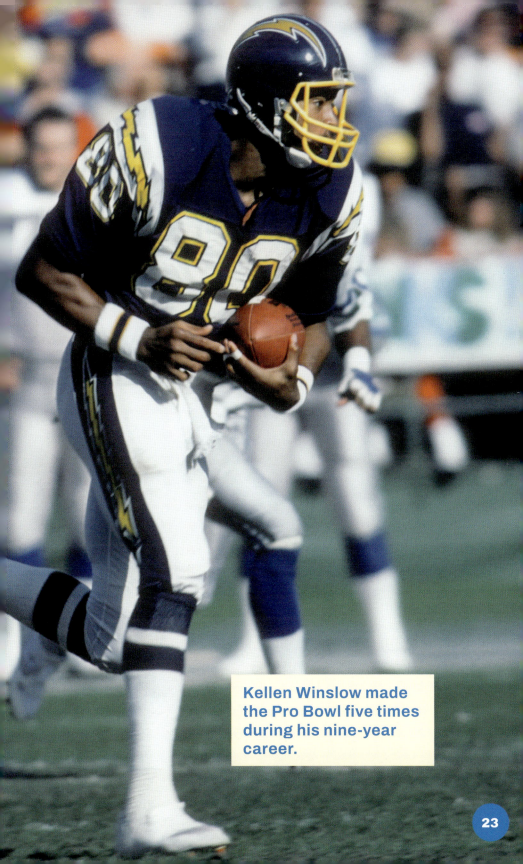

Kellen Winslow made the Pro Bowl five times during his nine-year career.

Cornerback Gill Byrd was a 10-year starter. He pulled down 42 interceptions during his career. Linebacker Junior Seau joined the team in 1990. He became the heart and soul of San Diego's defense. Starting in 1991, Seau made 12 straight Pro Bowls. Safety Eric Weddle joined the team in 2007. He was a five-time all-NFL pick.

BIG BLOCKER

Right tackle Ron Mix was a Charger from the beginning. He played for the team from 1960 to 1969. Mix was one of the best blockers of his era. He made the all-AFL first team nine years in a row.

Junior Seau (55) recorded 1,480 tackles in his 13 years with the Chargers.

Leslie O'Neal (91) racked up 105.5 sacks as a member of the Chargers.

Defensive tackle Gary Johnson recorded 17.5 sacks in 1980. That led the NFL. Defensive end Leslie O'Neal joined the team in 1986. That season, he was named Defensive Rookie of the Year. He later became the Chargers' all-time leader in sacks.

GETTING STARTED

Quarterback Drew Brees is best known as a New Orleans Saint. But he began his career with the Chargers. Brees spent four years as San Diego's starter. His best season came in 2004. He led the Chargers to the playoffs that year.

CHAPTER 4
RECENT HISTORY

Starting in 2006, San Diego won four division titles in a row. However, the Chargers often struggled in the playoffs. In the 2007 season, they made it to the conference title game. But the mighty New England Patriots ended their season.

Tight end Antonio Gates runs for extra yards during a playoff game in the 2008 season.

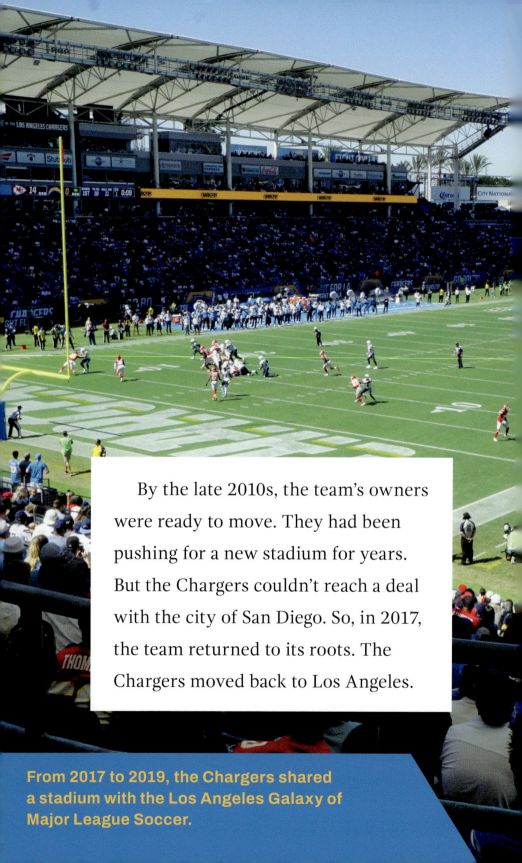

By the late 2010s, the team's owners were ready to move. They had been pushing for a new stadium for years. But the Chargers couldn't reach a deal with the city of San Diego. So, in 2017, the team returned to its roots. The Chargers moved back to Los Angeles.

From 2017 to 2019, the Chargers shared a stadium with the Los Angeles Galaxy of Major League Soccer.

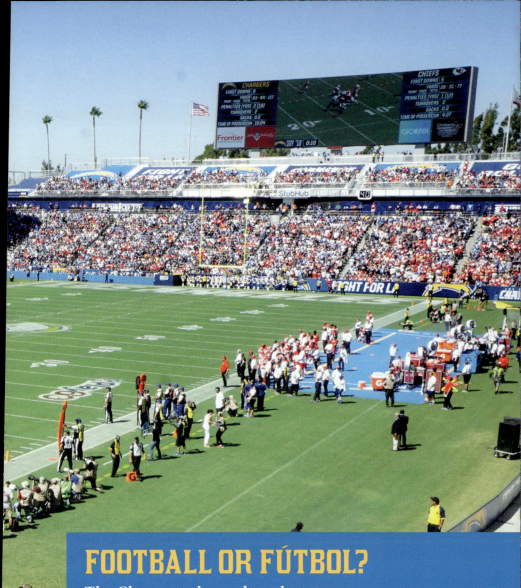

FOOTBALL OR FÚTBOL?

The Chargers planned to play at a new stadium in Los Angeles. But it would take a few years to build. So, from 2017 to 2019, the Chargers played at a soccer stadium. It held only 27,000 fans. Most NFL stadiums hold more than twice that number.

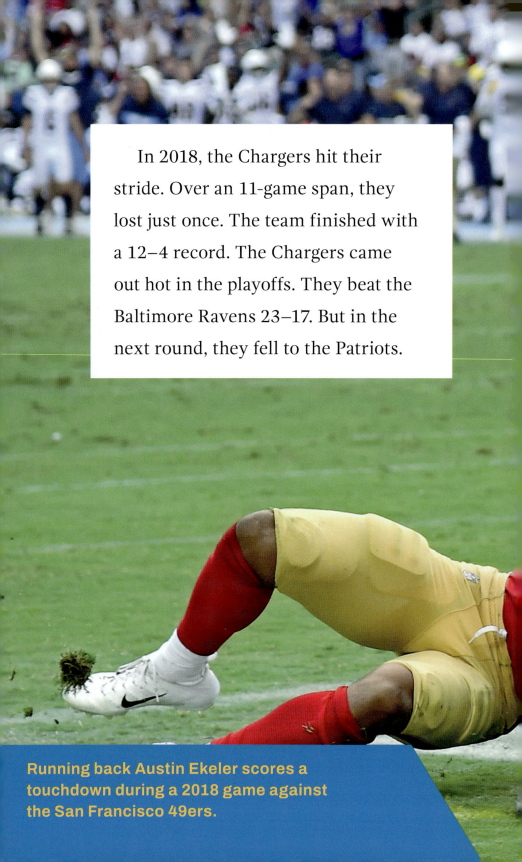

In 2018, the Chargers hit their stride. Over an 11-game span, they lost just once. The team finished with a 12–4 record. The Chargers came out hot in the playoffs. They beat the Baltimore Ravens 23–17. But in the next round, they fell to the Patriots.

Running back Austin Ekeler scores a touchdown during a 2018 game against the San Francisco 49ers.

Justin Herbert tossed 114 touchdown passes in his first four NFL seasons.

The next three years were a roller-coaster ride for the Chargers. Longtime quarterback Philip Rivers left the team. However, the Chargers welcomed an exciting rookie in 2020. Justin Herbert led the team back to the playoffs in 2022.

NEW COACH

The Chargers made a coaching change after the 2023 season. They hired Jim Harbaugh. Harbaugh had a proven track record. He led the San Francisco 49ers to the Super Bowl in the 2012 season. Then he led the University of Michigan to a national title in 2023. Fans in Los Angeles hoped Harbaugh would lead the Chargers to glory, too.

PLAYER SPOTLIGHT

LADAINIAN TOMLINSON

In 2001, the Chargers needed a running back. They selected LaDainian Tomlinson in the first round of the draft. Tomlinson was quick. He was strong. And he was a great pass-catcher.

Tomlinson topped 1,000 rushing yards in each of his first eight seasons. He could also find the end zone. In 2006, he scored 31 touchdowns. That set an NFL record. Tomlinson ran for 1,815 yards that season. He also won the Most Valuable Player (MVP) Award.

TOMLINSON SCORED 153 TOUCHDOWNS IN HIS NINE YEARS WITH THE CHARGERS.

CHAPTER 5

MODERN STARS

Quarterback Philip Rivers led the Chargers' passing attack from 2006 to 2019. The eight-time Pro Bowl pick was a fiery leader. He set many team records. Justin Herbert took over when Rivers left. Herbert earned the Offensive Rookie of the Year Award in 2020.

Philip Rivers started 224 straight games for the Chargers.

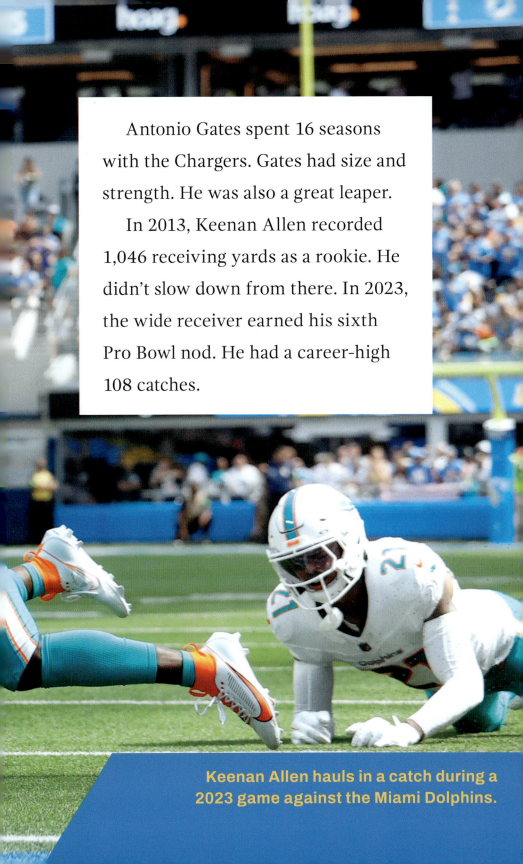

Antonio Gates spent 16 seasons with the Chargers. Gates had size and strength. He was also a great leaper.

In 2013, Keenan Allen recorded 1,046 receiving yards as a rookie. He didn't slow down from there. In 2023, the wide receiver earned his sixth Pro Bowl nod. He had a career-high 108 catches.

Keenan Allen hauls in a catch during a 2023 game against the Miami Dolphins.

Running back Austin Ekeler went undrafted in 2017. But he tried out for the Chargers. He made the team. Four years later, he scored 20 touchdowns. That led the NFL. Ekeler added 18 more touchdowns in 2022. Once again, that led the league.

DOING IT ALL
Melvin Gordon was the Chargers' top running back in the late 2010s. Gordon was a great runner. But he could also catch. He topped 1,300 total yards three years in a row.

Austin Ekeler looks for an opening during a 2023 game against the Green Bay Packers.

Defensive end Joey Bosa was named Defensive Rookie of the Year in 2016. He posted 10.5 sacks that season. The next year, he had a career-high 12.5 sacks. Safety Derwin James joined the team in 2018. He regularly made 100 tackles per season.

GOING STRONG

Linebacker Khalil Mack joined the Chargers in 2022. He was already a six-time Pro Bowler. But he was far from done. Mack kept up his dominance as a pass rusher. He posted a career-best 17 sacks in 2023.

Joey Bosa tallied 67 sacks in the first eight years of his career.

PLAYER SPOTLIGHT

JUSTIN HERBERT

The Chargers selected quarterback Justin Herbert in the 2020 draft. Herbert was big. He also had a strong arm.

Herbert didn't expect to play much as a rookie. But the team's starting quarterback got hurt. Herbert proved he was ready. He threw for 4,336 yards and 31 touchdowns in 2020. That helped him earn the Offensive Rookie of the Year award. Best of all, he kept improving. In 2022, Herbert led his team to the playoffs. Chargers fans hoped he was just getting started.

HERBERT TOPPED 17,000 PASSING YARDS IN HIS FIRST FOUR NFL SEASONS.

CHAPTER 6

TEAM TRIVIA

Early on, the Chargers wore powder blue jerseys. The team later switched to a darker shade of blue. But in 1994, the powder blues returned. The Chargers used them as a throwback uniform. In 2020, the team returned to powder blue as its main color.

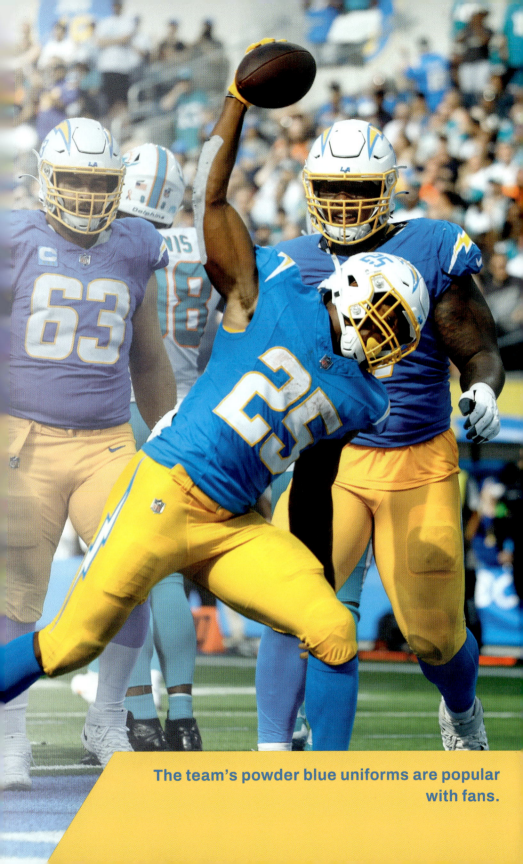

The team's powder blue uniforms are popular with fans.

The Chargers are known as the Bolts. One fan took his love for the team to an extreme. He made a Boltman costume. It had a lightning bolt for a head. The fan started wearing the costume to games. Before long, he became the team's unofficial mascot.

WHAT'S IN A NAME?

In 1959, owner Barron Hilton was deciding what to call his new team. At the time, the University of Southern California had a white horse as its mascot. Hilton knew fans loved watching the horse run across the field. A charger is another name for a horse. So, Hilton called his team the Chargers.

Boltman first appeared in the 1990s.

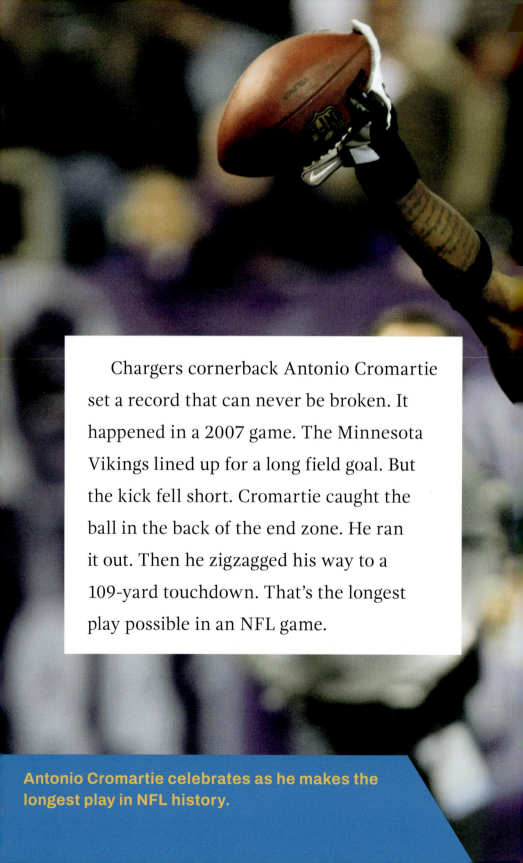

Chargers cornerback Antonio Cromartie set a record that can never be broken. It happened in a 2007 game. The Minnesota Vikings lined up for a long field goal. But the kick fell short. Cromartie caught the ball in the back of the end zone. He ran it out. Then he zigzagged his way to a 109-yard touchdown. That's the longest play possible in an NFL game.

Antonio Cromartie celebrates as he makes the longest play in NFL history.

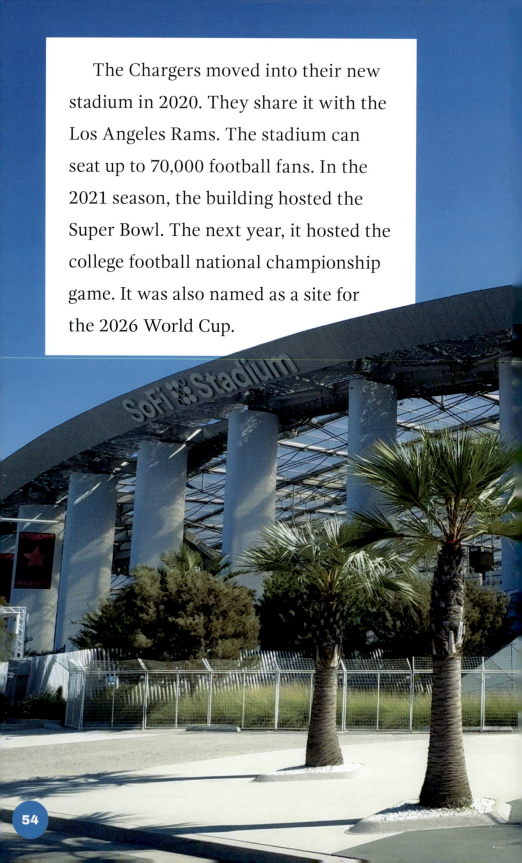

The Chargers moved into their new stadium in 2020. They share it with the Los Angeles Rams. The stadium can seat up to 70,000 football fans. In the 2021 season, the building hosted the Super Bowl. The next year, it hosted the college football national championship game. It was also named as a site for the 2026 World Cup.

The Chargers' stadium cost more than $5 billion to build.

TEAM RECORDS

All-Time Passing Yards: 59,271
Philip Rivers (2004–19)

All-Time Touchdown Passes: 397
Philip Rivers (2004–19)

All-Time Rushing Yards: 12,490
LaDainian Tomlinson (2001–09)

All-Time Touchdowns: 153
LaDainian Tomlinson (2001–09)

All-Time Receiving Yards: 11,841
Antonio Gates (2003–18)

All-Time Interceptions: 42
Gill Byrd (1983–92)

All-Time Sacks: 105.5
Leslie O'Neal (1986–95)

All-Time Scoring: 1,076
John Carney (1990–2000)

All-Time Coaching Wins: 86
Sid Gillman (1960–71)

AFL Titles: 1
(1963)

All statistics are accurate through 2023.

TIMELINE

1960 — The Los Angeles Chargers begin playing in the AFL.

1961 — After one season in Los Angeles, the Chargers move to San Diego.

1963 — The Chargers crush the Boston Patriots 51–10 to win the AFL title.

1970 — The AFL joins together with NFL. The Chargers become members of the AFC West.

1981 — The Chargers reach the conference title game for the second straight season.

1994 — The Chargers reach their first Super Bowl but lose to the powerful San Francisco 49ers.

2006 — LaDainian Tomlinson earns the league's MVP Award, and the Chargers win a team-record 14 games.

2017 — Team owners move the Chargers back to Los Angeles.

2020 — Justin Herbert takes over as the team's starting quarterback.

2024 — The Chargers hire Jim Harbaugh as the team's new head coach.

COMPREHENSION QUESTIONS

Write your answers on a separate piece of paper.

1. Write a paragraph that explains the main ideas of Chapter 2.

2. Who do you think was the greatest player in Chargers history? Why?

3. Which quarterback led the Chargers to their first Super Bowl?
   - A. Dan Fouts
   - B. Stan Humphries
   - C. Philip Rivers

4. Why was it unusual for the Chargers to play in a soccer stadium in the late 2010s?
   - A. Soccer fields and football fields have different shapes.
   - B. The Chargers did not have enough players on their team.
   - C. The stadium was much smaller than other NFL stadiums.

5. What does **era** mean in this book?

*He played for the team from 1960 to 1969. Mix was one of the best blockers of his **era**.*

- A. a great blocker
- B. a period of time
- C. a winning team

6. What does **dominance** mean in this book?

*Mack kept up his **dominance** as a pass rusher. He posted a career-best 17 sacks in 2023.*

- A. power over others
- B. a long season
- C. the end of a career

Answer key on page 64.

GLOSSARY

conference
A group of teams that make up part of a sports league.

division
In the NFL, a group of teams that make up part of a conference.

draft
A system that lets teams select new players coming into the league.

mascot
A figure that is the symbol of a sports team.

playoffs
A set of games played after the regular season to decide which team is the champion.

rally
When a team comes from behind.

rookie
An athlete in his or her first year as a professional player.

sacks
Plays that happen when a defender tackles the quarterback before he can throw the ball.

snap
The start of each play when the center passes the ball back to the quarterback.

throwback
Something that returns to the way it was in the past.

TO LEARN MORE

BOOKS

Coleman, Ted. *Los Angeles Chargers All-Time Greats*. Mendota Heights, MN: Press Box Books, 2022.

Stabler, David. *Meet Justin Herbert*. Minneapolis: Lerner Publications, 2024.

Whiting, Jim. *The Story of the Los Angeles Chargers*. Mankato, MN: Creative Education, 2025.

ONLINE RESOURCES

Visit **www.apexeditions.com** to find links and resources related to this title.

ABOUT THE AUTHOR

Brendan Flynn is a San Francisco resident and an author of numerous children's books. In addition to writing about sports, Flynn also enjoys competing in triathlons, Scrabble tournaments, and chili cook-offs.

INDEX

Allen, Keenan, 41
Alworth, Lance, 22

Bosa, Joey, 44
Brees, Drew, 16, 27
Byrd, Gill, 24

Coryell, Don, 12
Cromartie, Antonio, 52

Ekeler, Austin, 42

Fouts, Dan, 18, 20

Gates, Antonio, 41
Gillman, Sid, 11
Gordon, Melvin, 42

Hadl, John 20
Harbaugh, Jim, 35
Herbert, Justin, 7, 35, 38, 46
Humphries, Stan, 15

James, Derwin, 44
Jefferson, John, 22
Johnson, Gary, 27
Joiner, Charlie, 22

Mack, Khalil, 44
Mix, Ron, 24

O'Neal, Leslie, 27

Rivers, Philip, 35, 38
Ross, Bobby, 15

Seau, Junior, 24

Tomlinson, LaDainian, 16, 36

Weddle, Eric, 24
Winslow, Kellen, 22

ANSWER KEY:
1. Answers will vary; 2. Answers will vary; 3. B; 4. C; 5. B; 6. A